PUGS
IN COSTUMES

THOMAS DUNNE BOOKS.
An imprint of St. Martin's Press.

www.thomasdunnebooks.com
www.stmartins.com

The Library of Congress Cataloging-in-Publication Data is available upon request

ISBN 978-1-250-07575-8 (paper over board)
SIBN 978-1-4668-8717-6 (e-book)

St. Martin's Griffin books may be purchased for educational, business,
or promotional use. For information on bulk purchases, please contact
the Macmillan Corporate and Premium Sales Department at 1-800-221-7945,
extension 5442, or write to specialmarkets@macmillan.com

First published in the United Kingdom by Virgin Books,
an imprint of Ebury Publishing

First Edition: September 2014
First U.S. Edition: October 2015

10 9 8 7 6 5 4 3 2

PUGS
IN COSTUMES

THOMAS DUNNE BOOKS
St. Martin's Griffin
New York

PUGG

WOOD

Pugs of stage and screen

MARILYN PUG ROE

SUPER PUG

WIZARD OF PUG

PUGIANA JONES

CAPTAIN PUG

ELVIS PUGSLEY

MEMOIRS OF A GEISHA PUG

EDWARD SCISSORPUG

GONE WITH THE WIND

SCARLETT O'PUGRA

MR PUGAGI

PUG STORY

SNOW WHITE PUG

GANDALF THE GREY PUG

PUGS OF MIDDLE EARTH

MILEY WRECKING BALL PUG

BOB PUGLEY

TEENAGE MUTANT NINJA PUG

THE LION PUG

I DREAM OF JEANNIE PUG

THE INCREDIBLE PUG

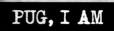
PUG, I AM

CHEWPUGCA AND PUG VADER

EVITA PUGRÓN

THRILLER PUGS

SWEET PUG O' MINE

I LOVE LUCY PUG

ROBIN PUG

THE VILLAGE PUGS

THE PUG OF WALL STREET

THE PUG OF THE BASKERVILLES

JACKIE O PUG

PUGe

VEEN

Trick or treat pugs

MOO PUG

AMELIA EAR PUG

PERCY PUG

PUGRITO

CHICKEN KUNG PUG

CINCO DE PUGO

COUNT PUGULA

SPIDER PUG

PUGLICE

SPORTS PUG

CLEOPUGRA

ANNA PUGLOVA

DINOPUG

BAT PUG

PIERROT PUG

PUGSTOCK

BEELZIPUG

LADYPUG

PUGCASSO

AMERICAN PUGBALL

PUGGERFLY

SCUBA PUG

SAILOR PUG

FROG PUG

BAD PUG!

GRAND NATIONAL PUG

PUGWATCH

PAWS

MARIE-PUGTOINETTE

ELEPUG

POPPY PUGS

ROYAL PUG

NIKKI PUGAJ

CALIFORNIA PUG

G.I. PUG

WOOLLY MAMMOTH PUG

BUSH PUG

LITTLE RED RIDING PUG

CAPTAIN PUGWASH

LOBSTER PUG

FRIDGE MAGNET PUG

AMERICAN EAGLE PUG

CHEER PUG

THE GOOD, THE BAD AND THE PUGLY

SENŌR PUG

MINNIE PUG

PEAPUG

FIREMAN PUG

MARVIN THE MARTIAN PUG

SQUIRREL PUG

ANGEL PUG

PEASANT PUG

ZEBRA PUG

TINKERPUG

BUMBLE PUG

BAILEY

PUG IN A PUG

UTURE

Best-dressed pugs in town

WEDDING PUGS

LOVE PUG

PIN-UP PUG

GLAMOUR PUG

PINK PUG

VIVIENNE WESTPUG

FAIRY PUG

BJORK PUG

PUGBACK MOUNTAIN

ST PUGRICK'S DAY

EASTER PUG

MAMA PUG

JAPUGNESE

PUG NO. 5

FLAPPER PUG

Picture Credits

Pg 6. Marilyn Pugroe – Kiwi – Janet Barrington

Pg 7. Superpug – Ben Koker / Oregon Humane Society

Pg 8 – 9. Wizard of Pug – Ivan and Roxy – Reuters / Mike Blake / Corbis

Pg 10. Pugiana Jones – Lightning– Paul Epps

Pg 11. Captain Pug – Russell Scheid

Pg 12. Elvis Pugsley – Jasper– Mandel Ngan/AFP/ Getty Images

Pg 13. Memoirs of a Geisha Pug – Mouchi and Olive – Richard Vogel/ AP/ PA

Pg 14. Edward ScissorPug – Sipa Press/ Rex Features

Pg 15. Pugerace – Kiwi – Janet Barrington

Pg 16. Scarlett O Pugra – Gracie – Timothy Clary/ AFP/Getty Images

Pg 17. Mr Pugagi - Blue - Phillip Lauer www.pupstarsonoma.com

Pg 18. Pug Story – Joe Blusys

Pg 19. Snow White Pug – Rick Harris / pugalug.com

Pg 20. Gandalf the Grey Pug – Blue – Phillip Lauer/ www.pupstarsonoma.com

Pg 21. Pugs of Middle Earth – Bono and Blue – Phillip Lauer/ www.pupstarsonoma.com

Pg 22. Miley Wrecking Ball – Tottie – McKenna

Pg 23. Bob Pugley – Roxy– Sue / Ruth Wedge

Pg 24. Teenage Mutant Ninja Pug – Ben Koker / Oregon Humane Society

Pg 25. PugZilla – Ben Koker/Oregon Humane Society

Pg 26. The Lion Pug – Douglas Smith / Getty Images

Pg 27. K–9 Pug – Ben Koker/ Oregon Humane Society

Pg 28. I Dream of Jeannie Pug – Kiwi / Janet Barrington

Pg 29. The Incredible Pug – Ben Koker/ Oregon Humane Society

Pg 30. Pug AM – Buster McKibben – Julia Shevchenko

Pg 31. ChewPugca and Pug Vader – Ben Koker/ Oregon Humane Society

Pg 32. Christina Pugilera – Kiwi – Janet Barrington

Pg 33. Evita Pugron – Mario Hagopian / Splash News / Corbis

Pg 34 – 35. Thriller Pugs – Rudy and Parker / Mario Tama/Getty Images

Pg 36. Sweet Pug O Mine – Blue – Phillip Lauer / www.pupstarsonoma.com

Pg 37. I Love Lucy Pug – Kiwi – Janet Barrington

Pg 38. Robin Pug – Bono – Phillip Lauer / www.pupstarsonoma.com

Pg 39. PlayPug – Maya – Erica Sommers

Pg 40–41. Village Pugs – Erica Sommers

Pg 42. The Pug of Wall Street – Pukster – Terry Alcorn / Getty Images

Pg 43. The Pug of the Baskervilles – Rainer Elstermann / Getty Images

Pg 44. Jackie O Pug – Kiwi – Janet Barrington

Pg 45. President Pug – Ben Koker / Oregon Humane Society

PUG O WEEN

Pg 48. Pugkin – Collette – Mario Tama / Getty Images

Pg 49. Moo Pug – Squishy – ZUMA Press / Alamy

Pg 50. Amelia Earpug – Jessica Furtado http:// allyouneedispug.com

Pg 51. Percy Pug – Hercules – Amy Conn/ AP /PA

Pg 52. Pugrito – Joe Blusys

Pg 53. Chicken Kung Pug – Ms Ping – Mario Tama / Getty Images

Pg 54. Cinco de Pugo – Kiwi – Janet Barrington

Pg 55. Count Pugula – Rick Harris / Pugalug.com

Pg 56. Spider Pug – Odin – Nick Savage / Alamy

Pg 57. Puglice – Soliel – AP/ PA

Pg 58. Sports Pug – Rick Harris / Pugalug.com

Pg 59. Cleopugra – Kiwi – Janet Barrington

Pg 60. Anna Puglova – Minnie –Rick Madonik / AP / PA

Pg 61. DinoPug Joe Blusys

Pg 62. Bat Pug – Boris – Paul Brown / Alamy

Pg 63. Pierrot Pug – FLPA / Alamy

Pg 64. Pugstock – Joe Blusys

Pg 65. Beelzipug – Archie – Dee McCracken

Pg 66. LadyPug – Lilly – Linda Lombardi

Pg 67. Pugcasso – Elmer – Sue

Pg 68. America Pugball – Boise Pug Meetup Group

Pg 69. Puggerfly – Little Buddha – Jill Hamilton – Krawczyk

Pg 70. Scuba Pug – Elmer – Sue / Ruth Wedge

Pg 71. Sailor – Bella – Erica Sommers

Pg 72. Frog Pug – Elliot – Allison Snider – Steve Kohls A /PA

Pg 73. Bad Pug – Odie – Enid Alvarez/NY Daily News Archive via Getty Images

Pg 74. Grand National Pug –Franziska Kraufmann / PA

Pg 75. Pugdini – Kiwi – Janet Barrington

Pg 76. Pugwatch – Blue, Roxy, Bono – Phillip Lauer www.pupstarsonoma.com

Pg 77. Paws – Lilly – Linda Lombardi

Pg 78. Gordon Pugzen – Riley Steven –Pugs and Kisses / www.pugsandkisses.com

Pg 79. Marie Pugtoinette – Sara Bogush

Pg 80. Elepug – Jessica Furtado www.allyouneedispug.com

Pg 81. Poppy Pugs – Mochi and Olive / Lisa Woodruff – Richard Vogel AP / PA

Pg 82. Royal Pug – Roxy – Phillip Lauer www.pupstarsonoma.com

Pg 83. Nikki Pugaj – Getty Images

Pg 84. California Pug – Roxy – Sue / Ruth Wedge

Pg 85. G.I. Pug – Pocky – Robyn Beck/AFP/Getty Images

Pg 86. Woolly Mammoth Pug – Rex Features

Pg 87. Bush Pug – Chia Pet Honeybear – John Chapple / Rex Features

Pg 88. Little Red Riding Hood – Richard Jones / Sinopix / Rex Features

Pg 89. Captain Pugwash – Tricky Fox – Paul Brown / Rex Features

Pg 90. Lobster Pug – Paul Brown / Rex Features

Pg 91. Fridge Magnet Pug – Harley John Chapple / Rex Features

Pg 92. American Eagle Pug – Izzy– Ben Koker / Oregon Humane Society

Pg 93. Cheer Pug – Elena Elisseeva / Alamy

Pg 94. The Good The Bad and The Pugly – Blue – Phillip Lauer www.pupstarsonoma.com

Pg 95. Senor Pug – Einstein – Paul Brown / Alamy

Pg 96. Minnie Pug – Jessica Furtado www.allyouneedispug.com

Pg 97. PeaPug – Maya – Erica Sommers

Pg 98. Fireman Pug – Phillippe Diederich / Getty Images

Pg 99. Marvin the Martian Pug – Kiwi – Janet Barrington

Pg 100. Squirrel Pug – Rick Harris / Pugalug.com

Pg 101. Angel Pug – Rick Harris / Puglalug.com

Pg 102. Peasant Pug – Sara Bogush

Pg 103. Zebra Pug – Jessica Furtado www.allyouneedispug.com

Pg 104. Rapugzel – Sara Bogush

Pg 105. TinkerPug – Bella – Erica Sommers

Pg 106. Bumble Pug – istock

Pg 107. Pug in a Pug – Bailey – Tina Moreau

PUG COUTURE

Pg 110. Wedding Pugs – Reuters / Rick Wilking / Corbis

Pg 111. Love Pug – Bailey – Tina Moreau

Pg 112. Pin–Up Pug – Chris Stein / Getty Images

Pg 113. Glamour Pug – Mamma Biscuit – www.mammabiscuit.com

Pg 114. Pink Pug – Clara Francis – Pugs and Kisses www.pugandkisses.com

Pg 115. Vivienne WestPug Mamma Biscuit – www.mammabiscuit.com

Pg 116. Fairy Pug – Clara Francis – Pugs and Kisses www.pugandkisses.com

Pg 117. Bjork Pug – Mamma Biscuit – www.mammabiscuit.com

Pg 118 – 119. Pugback Mountain – Roxy, Blue and Bono – Phillip Lauer www.pupstarsonoma.com

Pg 120. St Patrick's Day – Bandit – Gerald Brazell

Pg 121. Easter Pug – Clara Francis – Pugs and Kisses www.pugandkisses.com

Pg 122. Mama Pug – Jenny – Krystal Foster

Pg 123. Pug Life – Mamma Biscuit – www.mammabiscuit.com

Pg 124. Puganese – Penny – Robert Nickelsberg/ Getty Images

Pg125. Pug No. 5 – Mamma Biscuit – www.mammabiscuit.com

Pg 126. Flapper Pug – Gretta Rose – Pugs and Kisses www.pugandkisses.com

Pg127. Bah HumPug – Elmer and Roxy – Sue / Ruth Wedge